W9-BOB-444

ONE DIRECTION

One & Only

Publisher and Creative Director: Nick Wells
Project Editor & Picture Research: Polly Prior
Art Director and Layout Design: Mike Spender
Digital Design and Production: Chris Herbert

Special thanks to: Jane Donovan, Stephen Feather, Dawn Laker, Matt Knight

FLAME TREE PUBLISHING
Crabtree Hall, Crabtree Lane
Fulham, London SW6 6TY
United Kingdom

www.flametreepublishing.com

ISBN 978-1-4351-5764-4

Manufactured in China

1 3 5 7 9 10 8 6 4 2

'I do think it's quite scary, being known as a role model. We don't go around confessing to be role models or something like that. Because, you know, we might make mistakes in the long run.'

Liam Payne

Coming To A Screen Near You...

Their 3D movie *This Is Us* was a massive hit with fans when it opened in the summer of 2013, showing behind-the-scenes footage of the boys on the road as director Morgan Spurlock captured some of their most intimate moments on and off stage. All the footage in the feature-length film was genuine, showing how ordinary the boys can be: 'Nothing at all was scripted,' said Louis. 'If we are asked the question, we just answer naturally. I think that's the most important part, that we show people who we are. And to do that we can't have anything scripted, so it's all a reality.' As part of the marketing campaign for the film, fans were encouraged to upload pictures of themselves which would later appear on the poster. The film went on to top box office records and grossed over six times its budget. As for a sequel, One Direction fans will just have to wait and see.

Making Millions

1D may be millionaires (in 2014 they were revealed to be the richest boy band in British music history) and in demand all over the world, but the boys are determined to keep their feet on the ground, no matter how famous they become. Although they have played in front of sell-out stadia and the Queen of England, and appeared at the London 2012 Olympics Closing Ceremony, the lads credit their tight-knit families and close friends with making sure they do not let the adoration go to their heads. Thanks to that, One Direction may well take over the world, and we can be sure they will do it with cheeky grins on their faces. We can't wait!

The World At Their Feet

One Direction have defied even their fiercest critics and achieved what many assumed would be impossible: they have cracked not just America but Canada and Australia as well. Over the years, scores of boy bands have dreamt of making it big around the world, and record labels have invested vast fortunes in trying to promote their groups, including Take That and Duran Duran, but since The Beatles, few British boy bands have actually managed to achieve this. The lads are understandably proud because they have worked so hard to achieve their burning ambitions.

'My hopes for the future? To take over the world! You've got to aim high.' *Louis Tomlinson*

Going Global

Nothing the boys do is on a local scale. When they released their first DVD *Up All Night – The Live Tour* in May 2012, they sent fans into a frenzy by organizing a worldwide viewing party; the boys announced precisely when they would be watching the footage and tweeting along, while fans were encouraged to watch at home at the same time; the band-mates revealed all kinds of gossip and insider info from the show.

VIDEO
MUSIC
AWARDS
BROOKLYN 13
VIDEO
MUSIC

Online

onedirectionmusic.com:
Official site in many languages, with news, photos, events and more

myspace.com/onedirection:
Check this site out for One Direction's latest songs and videos

facebook.com/onedirectionmusic:
Find out what 1D are up to

twitter.com/onedirection:
Share your thoughts with the 1D boys and other Directioners @onedirection

instagram.com/onedirection:
Top photos and vids of your favourite five

raysofsunshine.org.uk:
Charity granting wishes to seriously ill children aged 3–18

Biographies

Nadia Cohen

Nadia Cohen is an entertainment journalist who has worked at a number of national newspapers and magazines, including *Grazia* and the *Daily Mail*. As a showbusiness correspondent, she covered film festivals, premieres and award ceremonies around the world. Nadia was headhunted for the launch of a new American magazine, *In Touch Weekly*, and spent several years living and working in New York. *In Touch* now has a readership of over a million, while Nadia lives in London and juggles family life with showbiz news and gossip. Previous titles for Flame Tree include *Justin Bieber: Oh Boy!*.

Mango Saul

Mango Saul has been a music, lifestyle and entertainment journalist for ten years. Some of his highlights include having breakfast at Waffle House with rapper Ludacris in Atlanta, sharing a bed with Destiny's Child for a *Smash Hits* cover interview and being sent an ice-cream costume for no reason. As editor of Sugarscape.com, Mango has seen the site grow to over 4 million page views per month and was shortlisted for Digital Editorial Individual 2011 at the AOP Awards.

Picture Credits

© Shutterstock: Featureflash: [illegible], 102; J. Stone: 1, 70; © Getty Images: Don Arnold/WireImage: 48, 85 Neilson Barnard: 10, 13, 64, 100, 112, 114; David M. Benett Entertainment: 93; Gareth Cattermole: 86; D. Dipasupil/FilmMagic: 6[illegible]; Stephen M. Dowell/Orlando Sentinel/MCT: 109; Fred Duval/FilmMagic: 7; Jon Furniss/WireImage: 8; Ian Gavan: 22, 46; Marc Grimwade/WireImage: 128; Jo Hale: 25; Dave J. Hogan Entertainment: 14, 38, 52, 62; Mark Holloway/Redferns: 58, 123; Hagen Hopkins: 21, 28, 106; Chris Jackson: 1; Jeff Kravitz/ FilmMagic: 30, 94; Michael Kovac/WireImage: 17, 22, 35; Scott Legato: 32; Stephen Lovekin: 105, 116, 124; Steve Mack/FilmMagic: 18; Danny Martindale: 118; Kevin Mazur/WireImage: Front Cover, 4, 7, 51, 90, 120; Marty Melville/AFP: 56, 96; Charles Norfleet Entertainment: 41; Joseph Okpako/FilmMagic: 26, 76; Al Pereira/ WireImage: 45, 69; Ryan Pierse: 80, 82, 98; George Pimentel/WireImage for MuchMusic: 78; Christopher Polk/KCA2012: 54; Debra L Rothenberg/FilmMagic: 74; Ilya S. Savenok: 42, 66; Lawrence Smith/Fairfax Media: 36; Stuart C. Wilson Entertainment: 3; Venturelli: 19; Theo Wargo/WireImage: 89, Back Cover; Kevin Winter: 110; Paul Zimmerman/WireImage: 73.

Discography

Albums

Up All Night (2011)
Take Me Home (2012)
Midnight Memories (2013)

Singles

2010: 'Heroes' (as *X Factor* 2010 finalists; UK No. 1)
2011: 'What Makes You Beautiful' (UK No. 1; US No. 4)
'Gotta Be You' (UK No. 3)
'Wishing On A Star' (with *X Factor* 2011 finalists; UK No. 1)
2012: 'One Thing' (UK No. 9)
'More Than This'
'Live While You're Young' (UK & US No. 3)
'Little Things' (UK No. 1)
2013: 'Kiss You'
'One Way Or Another (Teenage Kicks)' (UK No. 1)
'Story of My Life' (UK No. 4)
2014: 'Midnight Memories'
'You & I'

Tours

Up All Night Tour (2011–12)
Take Me Home Tour (2013)
Where We Are Tour (2014)
On The Road Again Tour (2015)

Awards *(including)*:

BBC Radio 1 Teen Awards

2013: Best British Single ('Best Song Ever')
Best British Group

Billboard Music Awards

2013: Top New Artist
Top Duo/Group
Top Pop Artist

BRIT Awards

2013: BRITs Global Success
2014: British Video ('Best Song Ever')
BRITs Global Success

MTV Awards

2013: MTV's Hottest Summer Superstar
MTV's Star
Best Song of the Summer ('Best Song Ever', VMAs)
Best Pop (EMAs)
Best Look (Harry Styles, EMAs)

Nickelodeon Kids' Choice Awards

2013: Favourite UK Band (UK)
Favorite Music Group (US)
Favorite Song ('What Makes You Beautiful', US)
2014: Favorite UK Band (UK)
Favorite Fan Family (Directioners)

NRJ Music Awards

2013: International Duo/Group of the Year
2014: Video of the Year ('Best Song Ever')
International Duo/Group of the Year

People's Choice Awards

2013: Favorite Album (*Up All Night*)
Favourite Song ('What Makes You Beautiful')
2014: Favorite Band

Teen Choice Awards

2013: Choice Music: Group
Choice Music: Love Song ('Little Things')
Choice Music: Single – Group ('Live While We're Young')
Choice Other: Male Hottie (Harry Styles)
Choice Other: Smile (Harry Styles)
Choice Summer: Tour (Take Me Home Tour)

World Music Awards

2014: World's Best Group
World's Best Selling British Artist
World's Best Selling Record Act
World's Best Pop Act

Further Information

ONE DIRECTION INFO

ONE DIRECTION

Niall

Birth Name: Niall James Horan
Birth Date: 13 September 1993
Birth Place: Mullingar, County Westmeath, Ireland
Height: 1.73 m (5 ft 8 in)
Star Sign: Virgo

Zayn

Birth Name: Zayn Javadd Malik
Birth Date: 12 January 1993
Birth Place: Bradford, England
Height: 1.75 m (5 ft 9 in)
Star Sign: Capricorn

Liam

Birth Name: Liam James Payne
Birth Date: 29 August 1993
Birth Place: Wolverhampton, England
Height: 1.8 m (5 ft 11 in)
Star Sign: Virgo

Harry

Birth Name: Harry Edward Styles
Birth Date: 1 February 1994
Birth Place: Holmes Chapel, Cheshire, England
Height: 1.8 m (5 ft 11 in)
Star Sign: Aquarius

Louis

Birth Name: Louis William Austin
Birth Date: 24 December 1991
Birth Place: Doncaster South Yorkshire, England
Height: 1.75 m (5 9 in)
Star Sign: Capricorn

VIDEO
MUSIC
AWARDS
13
·LOVE WILL TEAR US APART·

ONE DIRECTION

One & Only

NADIA COHEN

FOREWORD: MANGO SAUL, EDITOR, SUGARSCAPE.COM

FLAME TREE PUBLISHING

Contents

Foreword

Simon Cowell could see One Direction coming a mile off. Five young, good-looking chaps with reasonable singing voices and charm that would make any girl fall for them. TA DA! 1D were formed, as if by magic. The *X Factor* guru knew exactly what he was creating when he brought together Zayn Malik, Niall Horan, Louis Tomlinson, Liam Payne and Harry Styles – a boy band that were going to make him a ton of cash by selling millions of records. Globally.

Having the fastest-selling album of 2011 is a mean accomplishment. Being the first UK group to ever bag a No. 1 in the US *Billboard 200* is achieving the almost-impossible. Not even six-album Take That have mastered the US charts like One Direction have in just three. Actually, we need to forget Take That and any other boy band you can think of: we've not seen a pop phenomenon like One Direction since The Beatles and Beatlemania.

Some people may think that putting One Direction in the same sentence as The Beatles is complete madness, especially since the *X Factor* not-even-runners-up have only released two albums and a handful of singles. It's not madness. The band has charisma, good song writers behind them and, more importantly, Simon Cowell and his company Syco orchestrating the perfect pop machine.

If anyone thinks what One Direction have achieved so far is utterly amazing, we haven't seen anything yet. There's plenty more to come from this fresh new quintet...

Mango Saul

Editor, Sugarscape.com

DIRECTION

New British Invasion

In September 2010, the world had never heard of **Harry Styles**, **Niall Horan**, **Liam Payne**, **Zayn Malik** and **Louis Tomlinson**. The five boys did not even know each other's names and yet, within just 18 months of meeting each other, the singers – who joined forces to create the global phenomenon that is One Direction – had made history.

And on 21 March 2012, they became the first-ever UK group to debut at No. 1 on the American *Billboard* chart with their album, *Up All Night*. Previously, the highest entry for a UK group's debut was when the Spice Girls unleashed *Spice* in 1997; they had cracked America in style.

When One Direction heard about their record-breaking moment, they were in the middle of a jam-packed promotional tour across the States, causing pandemonium to break out wherever they went, as thousands of love-struck fans turned out for a glimpse of the biggest British group since The Beatles landed, almost 50 years earlier.

The Original Invasion

In December 1963, the CBS *Evening News* with Walter Cronkite ran a story on American TV about a new band called The Beatles, who were proving hugely popular in the UK, and played their hit single, 'She Loves You'. But what was intended to be a light-hearted news item sparked a frenzy across the

'We've got a lot of big dreams. We want to have No. 1s, travel a lot, go back to America and have as much fun as possible – I don't think that's too much to ask!'

Harry Styles

HARRY ★ NIALL ★ LIAM ★ ZAYN ★ LOUIS ★ HARRY ★ NIALL ★ LIAM ★ ZAYN ★ LOUIS ★ HARRY ★ NIALL ★ LIAM

nation: radio stations and record stores were flooded with requests for a record they did not have in stock, and when a DJ in Washington DC played 'I Want To Hold Your Hand', The Beatles' label, Parlophone, had no choice but to quickly release the record in the States – by then in the grip of a phenomenon which would become known as 'Beatlemania'.

'I Want To Hold Your Hand' reached No. 1 on the *Billboard* chart in January 1964, and when The Beatles appeared on *The Ed Sullivan Show* on 9 February, their position in pop history was secured. Forty-five per cent of Americans watched their now-iconic performance and, within weeks, Paul McCartney, John Lennon, George Harrison and Ringo Starr held the top-five positions on the chart – the only time any group has ever achieved that feat. The group's massive success continued on both sides of the Atlantic until they eventually broke up in 1970 due to internal tensions.

Making It Happen

Before they even set foot on American soil, One Direction were already superstars, thanks to clever use of social media. Executives from their label, Columbia Records, decided to use Facebook and Twitter for their marketing campaign instead of the usual strategy of releasing a single on the radio. Taking a gamble, co-chairman Steve Barnett decided to mount a four-month, word-of-mouth campaign with the intention of building a fan base before a single was ever

released or even played on the radio in America. Columbia asked fans to sign petitions and enter video competitions to win a concert in their hometown.

The gamble paid off spectacularly well and, within a few weeks, One Direction's Facebook page had 400,000 followers in the States. Their single 'What Makes You Beautiful' sold more than 131,000 copies, although it had yet to be played on the radio. In fact, radio stations were flooded with calls from fans demanding to hear their songs before the boys had even left London.

'It feels so strange when I look back to before The X Factor, when I didn't even have a passport and hadn't been outside the UK. Now all of a sudden I've been to all of these amazing places.'

Zayn Malik

Pandemonium Breaks Out!

One Direction's very first appearance on Canadian television in March 2010 was intended to test the water on the other side of the Atlantic. But few could have predicted the overwhelming reception the boys would receive. Officials were forced to shut down the streets surrounding the Toronto headquarters of Much Music when word got out that the band would be showing up. Thousands of screaming fans lined the streets behind the barriers and that was just the beginning. When they made their American TV debut on the *Today* show at the Rockefeller Center in New York City, 15,000 people mobbed the place. A few weeks later, more than a dozen hysterical Australian fans required first aid after passing out as the band were interviewed on Channel 7's *Sunrise* show in Sydney's central business district. The boys had also been due to perform a gig for Austereo radio station but the location was changed at the very last minute amid grave security concerns.

BBC
RADIO
ONE DIR

'When the day of the audition finally arrived, I decided I didn't want to go. I was lying in bed, refusing to get up, and it was my mum who told me I had to and made me get out the door!'

Zayn Malik

Getting Together

The boys all auditioned as individual contestants on the seventh series of ITV1's talent show *The X Factor* in 2010 and that was the moment when everything in their lives was changed for ever. That year, Simon Cowell was the mentor for the groups and declared himself 'genuinely very excited' about One Direction, who quickly became his best hope of winning the competition. Their performances provoked such loud screams from the studio audience that the judges' comments could hardly be heard. Amid all the hysteria, Simon confidently predicted his group were going to win: 'They get on well and they have steel in their eyes, and that's what I look for in my artists,' he noted. 'I think they'll go far.'

'The best moment for me out of the whole thing was when we were told we were going to be put in a band together, but I never for a moment thought that things would end up like this.'

Harry Styles

1D

The boys themselves were not completely confident of winning, but hoped to follow in the footsteps of JLS, who went on to build huge success from being *X Factor* runners-up in 2008. JLS's first single 'Beat Again' was a No. 1 hit in July 2009, and four months later their album *JLS* also debuted in the top spot. A headline tour and a BRIT Award swiftly followed, before another two bestselling albums, *Outta This World* (2010) and *Jukebox* (2011). Every time the JLS boys make a public appearance they are mobbed by legions of teenage fans – and have even complained about the girls' mothers making passes at them!

Auditioning Alone

Harry was already playing in a band called White Eskimo with some school friends when his mother Anne filled out *The X Factor* application form because he was too nervous. Liam had endured the audition process before, having first tried out when he was just 14, but only made it as far as the Judges' Houses stage that year. Louis also made a previous attempt in 2009, but didn't even make it through the first round. However, his rendition of 'Make You Feel My Love' (originally a Bob Dylan number, and later hugely successful for Adele) impressed the panel the following year. Niall prepared for his audition with a local *Stars In Their Eyes* show, where he was compared to Justin Bieber. Zayn was persuaded to give the show a try by his music teacher, Mrs Fox, who had already cast him in lead roles in several school productions, but he almost did not go through with it.

'To be thrown together like that and have to get to know each other was a bit scary. We're all quite different as well, so we did bicker occasionally. We get on brilliantly now, though. As soon as we were honest with each other it worked, and we've ended up being really close mates.'

Liam Payne

Meeting The Boys

All the boys did well at their individual auditions and made it through to the next stage – known as 'Boot Camp'. However, the competition in the boys' category was fierce and none of them was selected to move on to Judges' Houses until guest judge Nicole Scherzinger half-jokingly suggested they perform together, which would allow them to qualify for the groups category. They had only minutes to decide their future and choose a band name they would be stuck with.

Forming A Band

To prepare for the Judges' Houses stage of the competition at Simon Cowell's luxurious 20-bedroom villa in Marbella in Spain, the boys all went to stay with Harry's stepfather Robin in Cheshire and it was there that they started to form a bond. Of course they sailed through to the live shows and after the elimination of the other groups – F.Y.D., Diva Fever and Belle Amie – within four weeks, made it through to the final, in December 2010. They finished in third place, behind runner-up Rebecca Ferguson and the overall winner, Matt Cardle. Immediately after the final show, 'Forever Young' (the song they would have released, had they won) was leaked on to the internet and caused a sensation that would dramatically change five young lives for ever.

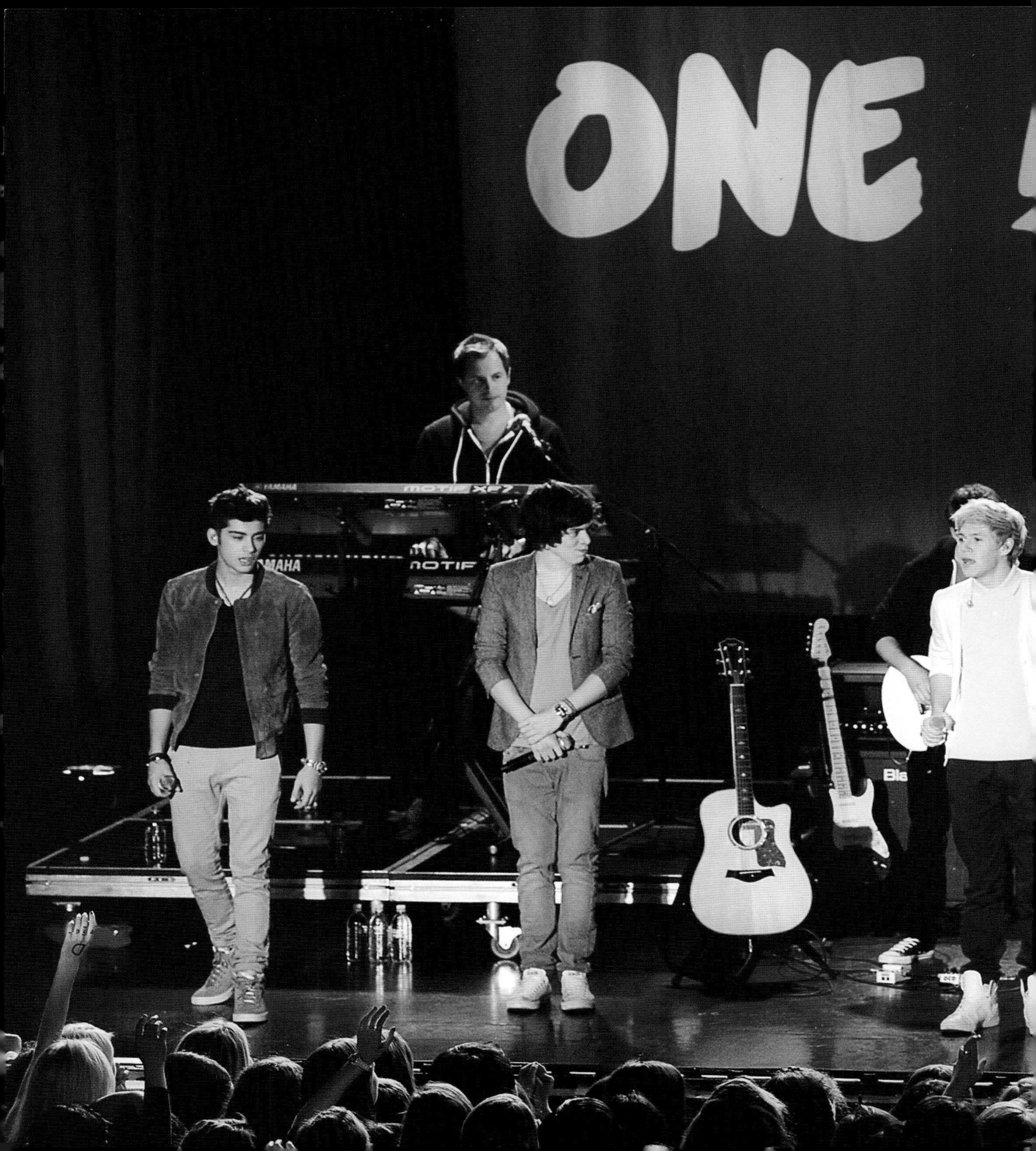
ONE
MOTIF XF7
YAMAHA
MOTIF

DIRECTION
EBS
1D
ONE DIRECTION

'We played a lot of gigs once the series finished and it was all new for me – I'd never even been to a nightclub before. I lived a very quiet, boring and sheltered life before the band, so absolutely everything that happened was a learning curve.'

Zayn Malik

Making Waves

When *The X Factor* final was over, the boys were devastated at missing out on the top prize and were all in tears until Simon Cowell called his favourite group into his dressing room, backstage at the Fountain Studios in Wembley, and made an announcement. 'You were great on the show,' he told them. 'Sony are going to sign you up in the morning. You're going to be all right, don't worry about coming third,' he added, before giving them all a hug, but urging them to keep the news secret until after Christmas.

In January 2011, One Direction signed a £2m record contract with Simon's company Syco before heading off to LA for five days to record some early tracks in the first professional recording studio any of them had ever seen. But there was no time to complete an album, for they were contractually obliged to spend the next three months on the X Factor Live Tour. The UK tour, which kicked off in February at the LG Arena in Birmingham, was a triumph.

X Factor Live Tour

The first time the boys hit the road together was alongside the other finalists from the show, travelling across Britain to perform to sell-out crowds. For One Direction, it was a taste of things to come as they were greeted by hordes of screaming girls at every venue. During the tour, the boys really started to forge strong friendships, carve out their image and along the way they gained a reputation for being pranksters, wrecking dressing rooms in Sheffield and Liverpool with messy food fights!

'We were completely **mobbed***. I was wearing a* **hoodie** *and* **half** *of it got* **ripped** *off me. Later, when we went to a* **book signing***, there was a* **girl** *who had brought the* **sleeve** *along to* **show me** *– and even* **asked** *me to* **sign it***! I thought it was* **hilarious***.'*

Louis Tomlinson

What Makes You Beautiful

When One Direction released their debut single on 11 September 2011, it broke the pre-order sales record for Sony Music. A week later, 'What Makes You Beautiful' stormed into the UK Singles Chart at No. 1, having sold 153,965 copies – the highest first-week sales for any song that year. It would remain at No. 1 in the UK and Ireland for four weeks. Days later, One Direction announced their debut UK dates and tickets for the Up All Night Tour were sold out within minutes of being released.

When the single was released in America in February 2012, it debuted on the *Billboard* Hot 100, going on to peak at No. 4 for two weeks.

'It was nerve-wracking, trying to find the first single, because of course we wanted it to be perfect. We all got to do a lot of co-writing, which was really important for us and we loved being involved.' Liam Payne

'Our aim with the album was to recreate the boy band sound, do something no one else is doing at the moment. We wanted some big songs that would surprise people; we wanted to be part of the writing process. We said from the word go that we wanted to be really involved, and we were very lucky that we got the chance.'

Niall Horan

Debut Album

One Direction released their first album *Up All Night* in November 2011, having developed it with producer Saran Pyrotechny in Sweden. It included collaborations with major stars, including Kelly Clarkson and Ed Sheeran, and was to prove a huge hit, following their relentless promotional schedule which included performances on popular television shows including ITV1's *Red or Black?*, BBC *Children In Need*, *BBC Radio 1 Teen Awards*, the *Jingle Bell Ball* at the O2 Arena in London and an appearance on the final of the eighth series of *The X Factor*.

Niall

Niall James Horan was born on 13 September 1993 in the small town of Mullingar, Ireland. Following his parents' divorce when he was five, Niall and his brother Greg split their time between the homes of their mother Maura Gallagher and dad Bobby Horan, before eventually deciding to live with Bobby when Maura remarried in 2005. Niall explained: 'I ended up moving in with my dad because he lived in town, so I had more friends there and it was more convenient for school and other stuff.' Although small for his age, Niall was a popular pupil at Colatitude Muire, a school for boys founded by the Christian Brothers. Although he did not excel academically, teachers recall that he was good at French and showed great potential.

'The simple fact is that I spent too much time messing about. I thought school was all about having a craic and acting like a fool.'

Niall Horan

'I'm 16 and I want to be a big name like Beyoncé and Justin Bieber. I've been compared to him a few times and it's not a bad comparison. I want to sell out arenas, make an album and work with some of the best artists in the world!'

Niall Horan, to X Factor judges at his audition

Musical Beginnings

Niall was into music from a very young age; at six years old, he started to play the recorder and took up the guitar aged 12. 'I was always the kid that picked up the nearest instrument and just loved music,' he recalls. His family first spotted his vocal talent when he was singing in the back of the car. 'My auntie said she thought the radio was on. Exactly the same thing happened to Michael Bublé with his dad – he's my absolute hero so I like the fact we have a similar story. My auntie said she always knew I'd be famous from then on, but I never thought anything of it.'

Before his big break, Niall was chosen as a support act for a previous *X Factor* contestant, Lloyd Daniels, when he performed in Dublin and was brimming with confidence when he himself auditioned for the show soon afterwards.

The Girls

Niall had a few teenage romances at school, but nothing lasted more than a few months, although he knew what he was looking for: 'I like the natural look and someone who can take a bit of banter, have a laugh, and who likes the same things as me – if you go out with me, you have to want to come to a football match. I support Derby County, and I always have.' Niall briefly dated *X Factor* finalist Amelia Lily in 2011, and has since been linked to singer Ellie Goulding and reality TV star Louise Thompson. But at the start of 2014 his

romance with stunning Hungarian model Barbara Palvin was so serious that he introduced her to his parents Maura and Bobby.

It was the first time Niall had ever taken a girlfriend home to Ireland, although that did not stop Harry trying to set him up with his sister Gemma Styles. Nor did it stop armies of admirers from trying their luck, although Niall has admitted to feeling overwhelmed by pushy crowds. Indeed he panicked the first time the boys were mobbed at Heathrow Airport shortly after *The X Factor* finished.

'I'm really **claustrophobic**, *so I was panicking a bit when we had to* **run** *through everyone and* **hide**. *I was so* **relieved** *when a* **police riot van** *came and got us – I still can't* **believe** *it happened, it* **feels** *like it was all some kind of* **mad dream**.'

Niall Horan

Heroes

Niall often says the best thing about being a star is having the chance to meet some of his favourite performers. Ed Sheeran has been a major influence, so when he collaborated with the boys on the song 'Moments' for their debut album, Niall was honoured and a little starstruck!

In the summer of 2013 Niall was thrilled to meet soccer star David Beckham backstage following their gig at the Staples Centre in LA: 'Met our footballing hero! Mr David Beckham!' Niall tweeted. 'He brought the boys and his little girl to see us! What a nice man! So courteous!'

'I was always into pop music when I was really young. I really liked Westlife, so to get to meet them and have a chat and a craic was brilliant. They were just laid-back and down to earth – must be an Irish thing.' Niall Horan

'It's amazing how word spreads about where we are. We do have to be a bit more careful because even if we just pop out to get something and people recognize us, it can go a bit crazy.'

Niall Horan

Zayn

Yaser and Tricia Malik were thrilled with the arrival of little Zayn Javadd on 12 January 1993. He grew up with three sisters in Bradford, where he attended Tong High School, and turned out to be rather a handful. 'I was quite hyperactive,' he recalled. 'I'd be bouncing off the walls and jumping from one room to the next. Even in the house, my mum used to put me in my pram because I was so full-on.'

But Zayn was a bright kid and by the age of eight he had a reading age of 18, as well as a talent for art and drama. He joined the school choir and was cast in productions of *Grease*, *Arabian Nights* and *Bugsy Malone*. Although he says he still feels like that kid from Bradford, Zayn is now recognized everywhere he goes and finds that difficult to deal with. 'I worry about being seen as a bad person,' he admits. 'Everyone makes mistakes, but when you're famous it's plastered everywhere. I want to be open, but I'm still learning about how open I can be and who I can trust totally.'

The Girls

Zayn credits the female influence of his three sisters Doniya, Waliyha and Safaa for making him good with girls: 'I was much more sensitive when I was growing up because I was around women all the time. I also think as a result I understand women more than the average man does,

ZAYN

to be honest.' After his first kiss at the age of 12, Zayn had his first real girlfriend when he was 15 and they were together for nine months. Since then, he claims, he's only had 'two or three proper girlfriends.'

Although Zayn has been linked to other women since *The X Factor*, he broke millions of hearts around the world in August 2013 by proposing to Little Mix star Perrie Edwards. Although initially the pair denied their romance, they have both since talked openly about their wedding plans (she suggested eloping to Barbados!). Smitten Zayn has even bought a house for his future mother-in-law Debbie. 'I wouldn't say I've got a specific type looks-wise when it comes to girls,' he says. 'I want someone who I feel comfortable around and I can spoil a bit; someone I can get on with. I've become a lot less shallow as I've got older and personality is very important to me now.'

'I absolutely loved being on stage and becoming somebody else. I found being a character really liberating and I used to get such a rush from acting.'

Zayn Malik

'Someone can be the best looking in the world, but if they're boring there's nothing worse – you have to have something to stimulate you mentally.' Zayn Malik

'A year ago, the thought of being on stage in front of that many people would have been enough to make me physically sick, but now I go out and walk around the stage and I feel so much more confident.'

Zayn Malik

The Rebel

The only member of the band who smokes, Zayn also has a huge collection of tattoos including a Yin Yang Tai-Chi symbol on his wrist, the word 'ZAP!' on his forearm, his grandfather's name 'Walter' in Arabic on his chest, a 'born lucky' symbol on his stomach, a silver fern on his neck and an inscription across his collarbone that says 'be true to who you are' in Arabic. He also has a wolf on his lower leg and an intricate sleeve tattoo of a crying eye with tears that transform into smoke and clouds around his right elbow.

Although he is close to the other lads, Zayn admits that from time to time, he gets frustrated with their pranks and untidiness: 'Having time alone is how I keep myself sane,' he says. And while he appears to have the world at his feet, Zayn suffers such bad stage fright that at one point during *The X Factor* he refused to go on stage to dance. In fact, Simon Cowell had to beg him personally to join the others as they learnt a basic routine. Zayn says: 'My confidence has improved so much since Boot Camp and I can have much more of a laugh with the boys about it all.'

In January 2012 he vowed to kick his cigarette habit, saying 'My New Year's resolution is definitely to quit smoking. I need to do it.' Although numerous Facebook pages were created to encourage the singer to quit, they have, so far, been in vain.

1D ONE DIRECTION THIS
WORLD PREN

ONE

Liam

Liam James Payne gave his parents, Karen and Geoff, quite a scare when he was born three weeks early on 29 August 1993 and needed resuscitation. As a result, one of his kidneys was scarred and dysfunctional. As a child, he endured 32 injections in his arm every morning and evening to cope with the pain. Now one kidney does not work and so he has to be careful not to drink too much – even water – and to stay healthy.

At school, Liam was something of an entrepreneur, buying boxes of sweets and selling them on for a profit, making himself around £50 a week. Although a sporty kid, he was bullied at school and took up boxing to learn how to fight back. 'I needed to find a way to defend myself,' he explains. 'I was, at 12 years old, fighting the 38-year-old trainer. I broke my nose, had a perforated eardrum and I was always coming home with a bruised, puffy face, but it gave me confidence. I got pretty good over the next couple of years.'

Musical Beginnings

As a child, Liam was always singing karaoke and joined the school choir when he was nine. He even won a solo, aged 13, when his choir joined with other schools to set a new world record for the number of people singing in unison. His mother Karen would juggle shifts as a nursery

'It was horrible to be turned away, but if I had made the live shows I wouldn't have known what hit me – I would have been gone straight away!'

Liam Payne

'My mates used to wind me up and pretend that girls liked me when they didn't, so I'd ask them out and they'd say no, which was mortifying.'

Liam Payne

nurse to accompany him on all his auditions and was by his side the first time he auditioned for *The X Factor* at the age of 14, wearing a pair of borrowed jeans (Armani, from his sister's boyfriend) and shoes with a hole in them (just old). He later explained: 'I didn't really have much of an interest in fashion generally, so when my first *X Factor* audition came around I had absolutely nothing nice to wear.' Liam waited nine hours to do the audition and eventually made it through to Judges' Houses, but Simon told him that he was not ready for the competition and asked him to come back in two years.

When he was 16, by then studying music technology at City of Wolverhampton College, Liam decided to give the show another try. 'I was the only one of the lads who really had to think about whether or not it was a good idea to become a band. I'd been working as a solo artist for so long that I couldn't imagine not doing that, but as soon as I made the decision to go for it, I knew I had done the right thing,' he explained.

The Girls

Although he landed his first girlfriend at the age of five, Liam did not always have such success with the ladies. A few years later, he asked the same girl out 22 times and she only agreed to go on a date after he sang to her! His audition song, 'Cry Me A River', was aimed at a girl who cheated on him.

When Liam started out in the show, he was dating his childhood sweetheart, Shannon Murphy, but their relationship fizzled out due to the amount of time spent apart. Liam then dated backing dancer Danielle Peazer for two years. They moved in together and even got themselves a dog, Loki, but went their separate ways in 2013, saying that their hectic schedules did not leave them enough time for a proper relationship. Not long afterwards, Liam hooked up with student Sophia Smith, whom he had known since they were at school together in Wolverhampton. After just eight months they broke up briefly, but appeared to be reunited within weeks.

The Sensible One

While the other boys tend to party pretty hard after coming off stage on a high, Liam admits that he prefers time to himself: 'I'm a fairly quiet person so I used to go to my room to be by myself. I've got a lot I want to achieve so drinking doesn't interest me.' Because of his kidney problems, Liam watches his diet carefully, particularly the amount of salt and protein he consumes, and prefers to unwind by working out in the gym. As a result, he has impressive six-pack abs to show for it and is happy to be known as the 'dad' of the group.

And when two of his band-mates were caught on camera, apparently smoking a joint in Peru in May 2014, Liam issued an apology on their behalf, saying they had 'a lot of growing up to do'. He tweeted, 'I love my boys and maybe things have gone a little sideways [and] I apologise for that. We are only in our 20s [and] we all do stupid things at this age.'

'I think even when I'm old enough to drink, I won't. My plan is to learn to drive so I can ferry the other lads around and act as security when we go out.'

Liam Payne

HA

Harry

1 February 1994 was the day when the world welcomed Harry Edward Styles to his family home in Holmes Chapel, Cheshire. His parents, Anne Cox and Des Styles, divorced when Harry was seven and they moved into the pub, run by Anne. 'That was quite a weird time,' recalled Harry. 'I remember crying about it. I didn't really get what was going on properly, I was just sad that my parents wouldn't be together any more.' He and his older sister Gemma were delighted when, five years later, their mother met Robin Twist.

At school, Harry was a keen badminton player, thanks to his father's enthusiasm for the sport: 'I liked the fact that it wasn't the most obvious sport to get into, and that you need quite a lot of skill to play it,' he says.

Musical Beginnings

Ever since he was at nursery school, Harry has loved performing to an audience and has appeared in productions of *Chitty Chitty Bang Bang* and *Barney*. He was also a keen singer and, when his grandfather, Harold, gave him a karaoke machine, he learnt all the words to dozens of Elvis Presley songs.

Harry was delighted when in 2006 he was asked to become the lead singer with a local band called White Eskimo.

Together with lead guitarist Haydn Morris, bass guitarist Nick Clough and drummer Will Sweeny, they won a Battle of the Bands competition. Following their success, they were asked to perform at a friend's wedding and were spotted by a music producer, who told Harry he reminded him of Mick Jagger.

'He's a mummy's boy – sometimes he phones up to five times a day.'

Anne Cox (Harry's mother)

The Looks

Harry is famous for his carefully coiffed hair and admits he has always taken pride in his much-admired appearance: 'My hair has changed a lot over the years,' he says. 'The worst thing was probably when I had blond streaks put in it when I was about eight. I thought it was cool when I went into school the day after having it done but looking back, I looked like a douche.'

Perhaps it helps that he is a big fan of naturism and was filmed naked several times while in *The X Factor* house.

'Now we were serious about carrying the band on and trying to get a deal one day. Being in front of an audience with the band had given me a taste for performing and I wanted to do more and more.'

Harry Styles

'Stripping off is very liberating,' he explains. 'I feel so free. It's always a spur-of-the-moment thing, but no one seemed to mind. I became a lot more confident during my time in the show and my confidence came out in my nakedness – I think you could safely say I'm not shy.'

The Girls

'It was a new experience for us all because it was like living in a student flat. We were just messing around, but it was a really good way of getting to know each other's personalities. We were learning little bits about each other by having silly banter.'

Harry Styles

Harry has a reputation for being quite a ladies' man and, unsurprisingly, was popular with the opposite sex from an early age: 'I wasn't one of those boys who thought girls were smelly and didn't like them,' he laughs. He dated several lucky girls at school, including Abi – whom he describes as his first serious girlfriend.

Since the end of his time on *The X Factor*, Harry has been linked to a string of women, including TV presenter Caroline Flack; their relationship sparked some controversy due to the 15-year age gap between them. His on-off romance in 2012/2013 with pop princess Taylor Swift provided her with rich song-writing material, resulting in her 2012 hit 'I Knew You Were Trouble'.

Harry adores his fans, and often takes them treats when he knows they have been waiting hours for a glimpse of him. He said: 'Some fans came to my house over Christmas, but I felt terrible that they were standing in the freezing cold because of me. We'll never complain about people coming to see us or wanting autographs or photos.'

OBSESSIO

There have been rumours swirling around his close friendship with Radio1 DJ Nick Grimshaw, but Harry tries to keep his private life as low-key as he can, and remains close to his mother Anne Cox – he was even best man when she married Robin Twist in June 2013.

'With some girls I may not find them attractive immediately, but then I really get to like them because their personality is so attractive. I like someone I can have a conversation with and I would always look for someone who could get on with my parents – it's important to me that my family like her too.'

Harry Styles

'I would never want to get bigheaded – it's such an unattractive trait and I can't imagine myself ever being like that. I always want to be aware of staying true to myself.'

Harry Styles

Louis

On Christmas Eve 1991, Louis William Austin arrived; since his parents, Johannah and Troy, split up when he was tiny, he took his stepfather Mark's surname, Tomlinson. He has six younger half sisters (Charlotte, Félicité, twins Daisy and Phoebe, Georgia and Doris) and a younger half brother (Ernest). As a child, he planned to become an actor and after finding himself an agent, he won small parts in the TV shows *Fat Friends*, *If I Had You* and *Waterloo Road*.

Louis attended acting school in Barnsley, South Yorkshire, but he was too busy having fun, filming and appearing in local plays, so ended up failing his first year of A-levels, following which he moved to a local comprehensive. He was always a hard worker and landed himself part-time jobs at Toys R Us and his local football stadium and cinema, but ended up being fired from the cinema after he failed to turn up for a shift because he was at his *X Factor* audition.

'Acting is something I would definitely think about pursuing later on, but for now it's all about the band.'

Louis Tomlinson

Musical Beginnings

At the age of 14, Louis joined a band called The Rogue, who had been looking for a singer. Alongside his friends, Geoff, Jona, Jamie and Stan, he performed for his class and gradually built up his confidence. At school, he landed the lead role in a production of *Grease*, which he looks back on with pride: 'I still get emotional when I watch the video because it was such a special time,' he says. 'I will never forget it.'

Louis was always a huge fan of Robbie Williams, and when Williams agreed to sing a duet of his hit 'She's The One' with the group for the live final of *The X Factor* in December 2010, all the lads agreed that working with the star was one of the highlights of the entire show. Louis says that Michael Jackson was also 'a real inspiration.'

The Girls

Louis has always had an easy way with girls, thanks to his sisters. 'When I was growing up, there were five women running around so I suppose in some ways it did teach me about women,' he explains. 'I'm certainly not intimidated by them because I'm so used to them!'

His first proper girlfriend was Hannah Walker, a primary school teacher from Doncaster, who made regular visits to London to support him during *The X Factor*. Two months after they split, he started dating politics student and part-time model,

'I really enjoyed performing and yet I never had the courage to do a whole school assembly because I was so intimidated. It's so weird to think that I've ended up performing in front of thousands!'

Louis Tomlinson

Eleanor Calder. Hannah said later: 'When I look at him on the television now I know him as two different people – one is the boy from Doncaster, and the other is Louis from One Direction.'

Despite the pair not being able to spend as much time together as they would like, Louis is still smitten with Eleanor, who is considered a calming influence on him.

'I absolutely love babies and kids. The boys are always taking the mickey out of me for how broody I am. I definitely, definitely want kids of my own one day.'

Louis Tomlinson

The Pranks

Louis first gained a reputation for being the prankster of the group when he left *The X Factor* studios wearing a hospital gown. When the boys were on the X Factor Live Tour in February 2012, he landed himself in trouble for wrecking dressing rooms: while in Sheffield, Louis tried to throw an apple core into the bin, but missed, which resulted in everyone throwing apples at the wall. A few days later, they did the same in Liverpool, but got away with it because they hid all the fruit in the shower and shut the curtains! He also has a reputation for constantly trying to trip the other boys up.

For a time, Louis and Harry rented a £3m London apartment previously owned by footballer Ashley Cole. They threw a New Year's Eve party at what they describe as their 'pimped-out penthouse' and Louis hired a coach to bring 50 of his school friends down from Yorkshire for the wild bash.

*'Every **now** and then, I get this **urge** to do some **daft stuff**. It all started with me **trying** to **throw** an **apple core** into the **bin**, which somehow turned into **everyone** picking up any **fruit** they could find. For those **five minutes**, it was so **much fun**!'*

Louis Tomlinson

'They're all *awesomely* talented *guys*, stupidly *good-looking*, of course. They've got everything, they've got the *whole package*.'

Tom Fletcher, McFly

Up All Night

One Direction's debut album – *Up All Night* – was released in the UK in November 2011 and four months later in the States, featuring 13 songs that the boys co-wrote with a series of top producers who had worked with Lady Gaga, Beyoncé and Britney Spears. They began work as soon as they had finished filming *The X Factor*, once Simon Cowell had signed them to Syco Music. Being runners-up on the show proved no barrier to success and the catchy first single from the album, 'What Makes You Beautiful', sold more than 100,000 copies in its first weekend and topped the iTunes chart within 13 minutes of being released.

The fastest-selling album of the year, it debuted at No. 2 in the UK and was only kept off the top spot by Rihanna's *Talk That Talk*. It went on to top the charts in Australia, Croatia, Italy, Mexico, New Zealand and Sweden, reaching the Top 10 in a total of 20 countries. The hysteria surrounding their first release led to comparisons with Westlife and Take That, who the boys all idolize.

The Songs

Up All Night opens with the up-tempo lead single, 'What Makes You Beautiful', and is followed by 'Gotta Be You' – a rock ballad that became the band's second single. The third

song, 'One Thing', was described by Syco Music as 'an epic pop smash-in-waiting, featuring soaring vocal harmonies, powerhouse guitar riffs and an anthemic chorus that refuses to leave your head.' Niall and Liam have said it's their favourite track on the album.

The fourth song, 'More Than This', is a slow ballad, and Harry's favourite. After that comes party anthem 'Up All Night', which namechecks one of the boys' favourite artists, Katy Perry. The sixth cut is 'I Wish', followed by 'Tell Me A Lie' – originally intended for Kelly Clarkson, who later said: 'I loved that they liked it – they sound really great on it.' After that comes 'Taken', then 'I Want', which was written by Tom Fletcher from McFly. The album finishes with 'Everything About You', 'Same Mistakes' and 'Save You Tonight'.

Critical Reaction

As well as the fans loving it, *Up All Night* also went down a storm with music critics, who raved about its anthemic pop songs and youthful lyrics about having fun and heartbreak. Allmusic's Matthew Chisling described *Up All Night* as a 'classic boy band album', adding that 'One Direction is perfectly positioned to take the world by storm'. Digital Spy's critic Robert Copsey called it 'an adorable as expected debut, with a surprising amount of bite,' while the *Daily Star* awarded it eight out of 10, saying that 'the lads' big personalities shine through on its belting fun pop anthems.

SUPRA FOOTWEAR
MUSKA 001

The boys were thrilled when 'What Makes You Beautiful' won the BRIT Award for Best British Single at the 2012 ceremony at London's O2 Arena, although in the excitement Harry accidentally thanked Radio 1 instead of Capital Radio, whose listeners had voted for the winner, and their music was briefly banned from the station. The band-mates also forgot to thank their parents, but that did not stop the boys from celebrating the huge popularity of their song.

The first three singles taken from *Up All Night* went straight into the UK Top 10 and 'What Makes You Beautiful' became the most pre-ordered single in Sony Music Entertainment history. It also topped the charts in Australia and New Zealand, the Flemish Ultratop 50 and the Canadian Hot 100.

The Tour

In September 2011, to coincide with the eighth series of *The X Factor*, the team at Syco came up with a clever way to hook young fans: they had to complete a challenge on the official One Direction website to unlock the album title and cover, which showed the band members on the beach.

When they announced 24 tour dates, the tickets sold out within minutes. The shows kicked off in Watford on 18 December 2011, ending in Belfast a month later. Then it was announced that there would be an Oceania leg of the tour, with dates across Australia and New Zealand set for April 2012, followed by 27 dates in America.

'We've got some great songs on the album, which show off all our voices.'

Louis Tomlinson

MUCH
MUCH
MUCH

Take Me Home

In November 2012, a year after the UK release of *Up All Night*, the boys were thrilled to bring out *Take Me Home*. Released globally, rather than region by region, it meant that they did not have long to wait to learn that they had scored another hit. *Take Me Home* went straight to No. 1 in over 35 countries, and sold over 1 million copies in its first week. They became the first boy band in US chart history to achieve two No. 1 albums in one calendar year.

The title of the new album was 'leaked' by Louis in August when he included the hashtag #takemehome in one of his tweets. Fans, predictably, went bonkers, retweeting #takemehome every few seconds.

'Everyone's said that second albums are the hardest, so before we started recording we were a bit nervous.'

Harry Styles

'We always want to push for as much writing as possible because we want it to sound as real and as genuine as possible. It's really important for us to be part of that writing process. We hope to do more with every album.'

Living It Up

'Live While You're Young' was the eagerly anticipated first single from the boys' new album. Released in September 2012, the song was a top 5 hit around the world. Written by same trio of Rami Yacoub, Carl Falk and Savan Kotecha who had penned One Direction's first hits, 'What Makes You Beautiful' and 'One Thing', the single was not without its critics, many of whom claimed that it lifted a riff from the intro of The Clash's 'Should I Stay Or Should I Go?'.

The video for the song was filmed at a 'secret place' in Kent, UK, and featured the quintet camping, playing football and generally frolicking around at a pool party with a giant microphone and an inflatable banana. Needless to say, upon official release, the clip was viewed 8.24 million times in just 24 hours, breaking the previous record set by Justin Bieber's 'Boyfriend' of 8 million views in 24 hours.

A Good Thing

'Little Things', an Ed Sheeran penned heart-tugger, was released in the UK at the same time as the album, making the boys the first band to land a No. 1 in both the single and album charts at the same time. The song is accompanied by acoustic guitar, which, in the video, is provided by a confident Niall. They even played it to the Queen, at the 2012 Royal Variety Performance.

'As soon as we started recording music, we were aware that people would be surprised by it because it's not typical boy-band music. There's nothing else out there like our sound at the moment, it's completely new – it's One Direction's sound and we love it!'

Zayn Malik

Friends and Collaborators

Although their new album featured many veteran songwriters and producers, the boys were very proud of the fact that they co-wrote many of the tracks. The song, 'Back For You' was particularly poignant for Louis, who said that it was 'the one we wrote the majority of the lyrics for... It's all about being away on tour and missing our girlfriends.' The boys particularly enjoyed working with the likes of McFly's Tom Fletcher, and also with Ed Sheeran, with whom they not only recorded songs, but, according to Niall, had watermelon fights.

'We miss home a lot, but we love being on the road.'

Niall Horan

Around The World

Before their 2012 tour was even over, the boys were already announcing plans for another one, to start in February 2013. Selling out in minutes, extra dates were added to an already gruelling schedule between February and October, making their 2013 World Tour a total of 117 shows in Europe, Australasia and North America. And to top it all, the boys no longer had to behave like mere mortals and queue at airports, but were instead ferried between venues in their very own luxury private jet, dubbed Air Force One Direction.

Midnight Memories

There was a widespread frenzy of hysteria when the boys announced in the summer of 2013 that not only were they starting work on their eagerly anticipated third studio album but that its release would also coincide with a third world tour, the Where We Are Tour.

Despite a mixed reaction from music critics, the fans adored *Midnight Memories* when it was released in November 2013, snapping up copies within hours. It immediately became the fastest selling album in Amazon's 15 year history, and hit the US chart at No. 1, making 1D the first group ever to debut at the top spot with their first three albums. In the UK it sold 187,660 copies in just the first four days, outselling releases the same week by well-established stars including Gary Barlow and Michael Bublé. It also outsold the band's own previous two albums, and was declared the global bestseller of 2013 when it had sold four million copies in just five weeks.

Before the entire album was unveiled, two singles, 'Best Song Ever' and 'Story Of My Life', were released in July and October 2013, both shooting straight to the top of the charts – but the boys teased their fans by not announcing the album's title until the last minute.

What's In A Name?

First Niall gave the heads up when he tweeted that they had an exciting announcement. Then Zayn posted a five-second

US APART

teaser video of Harry spelling out the letters 'M I D' with alphabet cards, which had fans frantically trying to decipher the name. Not long after, that was followed by a full video showing Harry completing the puzzle and giving two thumbs up on the band's hugely popular Instagram account.

According to critics, the album was generally considered to have more rock'n'roll elements than their previous releases, which were filled with catchy songs about being young and in love. 'It's a very rock direction,' Liam agreed. 'We actually spent a lot of time writing this album. We're very proud of it so we are hoping people will kind of adjust to the music with us.' 'Midnight Memories' and 'You & I' were two other tracks from the 14-track record to be released officially worldwide as singles, both with typically action-packed accompanying videos.

'The boys want to be honest about their age and their situation as young men. They aren't the naive, clean-cut guys next door any more – they're rock stars and this new record will reflect that.'

Julian Bunetta, 1D's songwriter

Life On The Road

The Where We Are Tour kicked off at El Campín Stadium in Bogota, Colombia, on 25 April 2014, with a performance the *Mirror* described as 'stunning'. Live streams across the globe crashed due to the sheer volume of fans trying to catch the show. The 40,000 strong crowd loved every minute of the boys' performance: many fans were spotted screaming and crying or waving glowsticks as the gig kicked off with 'Midnight Memories'. They played a further 68 shows, performing to capacity crowds in stadia across Europe and North and South America.

'On the third record, we've kind of broken up into our little camps of who we work well with, and I work well with Liam. It's great to have a lot more involvement and control.'

Louis on writing Midnight Memories

The excitement continued when the band confirmed dates for a fourth epic tour, the On The Road Again tour, which would see them performing in the Middle East for the first time in April 2015. Following months of discussion they arranged to stage a concert at The Sevens Stadium in Dubai: 'We can't wait to meet all our Middle East fans when we perform in Dubai,' said Zayn in a specially recorded video message. As well as the Dubai concert the tour was also set to include dates in Australia, Asia and South Africa.

'If the demand's there then we're always willing to come,' Louis said about their relentless travel plans. 'It's just something to work out with the different locations.'

The band's mentor, music mogul Simon Cowell, praised the band for coping with the stress of being constantly on the road touring: 'They are amazingly nice boys considering how much their lives have changed,' he said. 'It's very difficult because when they're in the situation they're in, where literally the whole world wants you to perform, you've got this opportunity in your life and it's very difficult to turn it down.'

'We all have different tastes, [but] they all seem to come together to make a One Direction song.' Niall Horan

MOTIF
Blockstar

DIRECTION
DIRECTION
EBS

Here's Looking At You

Being catapulted from total obscurity into a world of superstardom where their every move is watched, discussed and analysed by armies of adoring fans has proved an overwhelming experience for Harry, Zayn, Liam, Niall and Louis. Although some moments are pretty hair-raising, especially when mobbed by huge crowds, the boys are getting used to the glare of the spotlight. The first time they flew into Heathrow Airport together after *The X Factor*, they were stunned by the enormous throng of girls waiting for them.

The Entourage

Harry admits it can be a struggle keeping his feet on the ground when surrounded by an entourage of staff. Their stylist, Caroline Watson, has helped them find their own look: 'The boys are all quite individual in their styles,' she says. 'I've tried to carve out an identity in their style for them, which they all love and are really growing into.' Hairdresser Lou Teasdale has been a constant presence, ensuring the band-mates are always perfectly groomed. She said: 'I would shave Liam's head and grow Zayn's long. I'm not winning on either. My favourite hair is Louis' because it's got really long and he lets me do fun stuff with it.' Celebrity bodyguard Jacquie Davies watches their backs. She said: 'It would have been so easy for them to go down the spoilt brat route, having found fame so young, but they are the complete opposite – lovely, polite boys, who are an absolute pleasure to work with.'

'There was literally a wall of fans. I got hit in the face by mistake in the scuffle and some of the other lads had clothes ripped off. Someone had hold of my hood, so I ended up being squashed up against the side of the van – it was all quite dramatic.'

Liam Payne, after being mobbed by fans

'I'm trying my ***best*** *to stay as* ***down-to-earth*** *as possible* ***so*** *I don't want people doing* ***things*** *for me that I could do* ***myself.*** *I'm capable of* ***picking up*** *my own* ***water****, so why should* ***they*** *have to do* ***it****?'* *Harry Styles*

The Image

While millions of girls want to be with them, just as many boys want to look like One Direction and high streets everywhere are now full of lookalike fashions. After they were spotted in *The X Factor* house wearing distinctive onsies, the Oslo-based designer OnePiece, sold out of the garments in days. It has been good news for Toms, makers of the eco-friendly shoes worn by Louis, and sales of the Fred Perry tennis trainers Niall prefers have also surged. Harry is often to be found on the FROW at London or New York's Fashion Weeks; his appearance at LFW's Aquascutum show resulted in the classic British label becoming cool all over again, and his donning of a heart-print Burberry shirt influenced many a copycat wearer, including the Queen of Fashionistas herself, Victoria Beckham.

'I want to sit on Harry Styles' lap! I have a total crush on him. I like his curly hair and he looks like a little cherub.'

It-girl Poppy Delevingne

The Bodies

Since their fans like almost nothing better than when the boys reveal an inch or two of naked flesh, the band-mates have to make sure they are honed and toned to perfection. That means hours spent working out in the gym, whether they like it or not.

While on tour in 2013 they enlisted the help of professional trainers Mark Jarvis and Jimmy Wallhead who put the boys through their paces with boxing classes and circuit training. Luckily the boys all love sport – they released footage of themselves working out: Niall was seen straddling a weights machine, which focused on his shoulders and back, Harry was on the treadmill, and Liam revealed he was taking protein shakes to build up more muscle. Although the team tried to enforce strict low-carb diets, they would have had their work cut out seeing as all the boys love pizza and Nandos' chicken, while Louis' favourite food is a bacon, egg and cheese sandwich dipped in brown sauce!

'I ask Niall if he wants to go to the gym and he says, "I'll see you there," then never turns up – unless he's hiding under the weight bench, lifting 40 kg and I didn't spot him!'

Liam Payne

1D THIS IS US
PROD .NO.
SCENE
TAKE
DATE
SOUND
DIRECTOR
CAMERAMAN
1D THIS IS US
PROD .NO.
SCENE
TAKE
DATE
ROLL
PROD .C O.
DIRECTOR
SOUND
CAMERAMAN

1D THIS IS US
PROD .NO.
SCENE
TAKE
ROLL
DATE
SOUND
PROD .C O.
DIRECTOR
CAMERAMAN
1D THIS IS US
PROD .NO.
SCENE
TAKE
ROLL
DATE
SOUND
PROD .C O.
DIRECTOR
CAMERAMAN

'We've met some amazing children through working with Rays of Sunshine and feel honoured to be in a position to help. The charity gives thousands of seriously ill kids the chance to take time out and have some fun, and we are delighted to help wherever we can.'

Zayn Malik

We Love You

It should come as no great surprise that the boys have some very famous fans, including America's First Lady, Michelle Obama, who is so smitten that she invited them to the annual Easter Egg Hunt at the White House, held on Easter Monday 2012. Unfortunately, their hectic promotional schedule did not allow the visit, but they cheekily asked if they could come back another time. They have also caught the eye of Arnold Schwarzenegger's daughter Katherine, though Harry is perhaps understandably wary of the *Terminator* star!

Fellow musicians Lily Allen, Lady Gaga and Coldplay's Chris Martin are all 1D fans, and the boys also proved a hit with the notorious Kardashians. In March 2012, Niall tweeted Khloe, inviting her to attend a concert for 7,000 fans in Dallas, and just a few weeks later, Harry made a blatant attempt to grab her sister Kim's attention by turning up to an interview in the States, holding a massive poster of her in a bikini with a Post-It note attached, saying: 'Call me, maybe?' He ended up briefly dating her younger sister Kendall but the direct approach had certainly worked in the past when he wooed his ex-girlfriend Caroline Flack by shamelessly posing with a sign that read: 'To Flackster! Never too old. Let's make it happen!! Lots of love, Harry S'.

'Imagine having Arnie as your dad-in-law!' Harry Styles

Popularity Contest

Since Harry is easily the most adored band member in the UK and has more Twitter followers than the others, the plan was to make him the lead singer as most boy bands in the States have a recognized frontman. Initially, he was given leading roles, however across the Atlantic, Niall has found himself more popular than the others. US fans seem to love his All-American looks, so much so that Simon Cowell banned him from dyeing his blond hair. Although pursued by excited admirers wherever he goes, Niall insists he is not much of a ladies' man, but that has not stopped American singer-songwriter and actress Demi Lovato from declaring her affection: 'He's so adorable!' she said. When quizzed on a possible romance, Mr Horan admitted: 'I'd like to see her all right and she's a similar age.'

'I would like to carry on what we're doing and get bigger, better and stronger. I want to go everywhere and do everything!'

Niall Horan

Charity Work

The boys may now be superstars, but they're not letting all the attention go to their heads and still insist on helping others as much as they can. In 2011, together with other *X Factor* finalists, they recorded a cover of Rose Royce's 'Wishing On A Star' for the children's charity Together For Short Lives, and their 2013 Comic Relief single 'One Way Or Another (Teenage Kicks)' was not only a No. 1 hit in the UK, but it helped to raise £2 million for the charity. One Direction are also ambassadors for the charity Rays of Sunshine, which grants

'I've not actually been on too many dates. I just like sitting at home, chilling and watching a movie.'

Niall Horan

wishes for seriously ill children between 3 and 18 years old; they often visit patients at home, and invite special fans backstage. They did just that in June 2014 when, before going on stage at Wembley Stadium during their Where We Are Tour, they met children living with serious or life-limiting illnesses, answered their questions and posed for photos.

The Doubters

It's almost impossible to imagine anyone not liking the adorable quintet, but the boys have managed to make one or two enemies along the way. Indeed, they were almost sued by an American group, who claimed they owned the name first. In April 2012, the US One Direction filed a lawsuit, asking for a court order to force the British band to change its name. In the legal documents, the American band (also made up of five cute boys) says it formed in 2009, a year before Niall, Zayn, Liam, Harry and Louis had even met. However, the matter was settled, with the British One Direction keeping their name.

The 1D boys are also noted for their frequent online 'rants', posting about anything (or anyone) that gets them hot and bothered. They also used to enjoy Twitter feuds with fellow boy band, The Wanted, and were reported saying it was 'a shame' their chart rivals were no longer around to argue with online. The rows were 'quite enjoyable,' said Liam.

'As a band, we're having the absolute best time ever. We've become better friends than I could ever have imagined and it's so nice to have four other lads to share this experience with. I think we're going to get tighter and tighter as time goes on.'

Harry Styles

The Directioners

Dedicated fans are known as 'Directioners' and they are so devoted to the boys' happiness that one girl from Boston was distraught when it rained in her hometown during the band's visit – in case it meant they would never come back! 'One Direction are in my city,' said Megan Connor, 'which means that I am breathing the same air as them.'

With girls permanently camped outside their homes and hotels, it seems they are living every young man's dream; Harry admits that it can be a struggle not to let all the adoration go to their heads. 'We get a lot of praise,' he says. 'Obviously it's lovely to hear and it always puts a smile on your face but I want to keep my feet on the ground as much as possible.'

Dealing With the Fans

For such young lads, One Direction have shown surprising maturity when it comes to dealing with the lavish attention they receive from exceptionally eager fans. Despite girls throwing themselves at Harry, Niall, Zayn, Liam and Louis, they are careful who they choose to hang out with and make sure they are not caught in compromising positions with girls they barely know.

'We have the most unbelievable fans,' says Niall. 'When we were staying in a hotel in Richmond, girls were outside in

'We have had to use the hotel service lift. There are girls in the main lift the whole day, just going up and down, hoping to bump into us!'

Harry Styles

'It can be strange – waking up to people screaming at 7am – but we love it!'

Liam Payne

sleeping bags or booking into rooms on the same floor as us. And every day after school, there would be about 400 or 500 fans there.'

In France, soldiers were called in to clear an exit route for the band as they attempted to board the Eurostar train at Gare du Nord, and in LA, where the boys bagged their own TV show on the Nickelodeon channel, they were forced to use back doors and secret entrances.

The Presents

The boys are constantly lavished with gifts, including carrots and cereal! Ever since Louis once joked that he loves girls who like carrots, he has been inundated with carrot banners, T-shirts and, of course, real vegetables. And while Liam receives licorice, Harry gets olives (as an ironic joke, even though he hates them) and one fan actually presented the group with portraits of their faces painted on Portobello mushrooms!

Jealous Frenzies

After Harry hooked up with presenter Caroline Flack during their stint on *The X Factor* and the couple were spotted on a date at London's St Martin's Lane Hotel in November 2011,

she was besieged with online abuse and received a slew of death threats. However, Harry inflamed the situation still further: when asked which of the contestants was his favourite, he referred to the 15-year age gap between himself and Caroline, saying: 'They're all a bit young for me.' Caroline was said to be terrified by the abuse and it only stopped when they split up in January 2012.

Emma Ostilly, another of Harry's former flames, also became a target for bitter fans after she started dating the star, and had to close down her Twitter account after receiving online abuse.

Liam's now ex-girlfriend, dancer Danielle Peazer, also endured death threats and name calling from jealous fans, but did little to stop the nasty bullying when she tweeted a photo of herself sunbathing in LA with a topless Liam by her side, in a move which inevitably made his fans green with envy.

Hi One Direction fans! To clarify. I'm close friends with Harry. He's one of the nicest people I know. I don't deserve death threats:) x

Caroline Flack, via Twitter, November 2011

'One night, two girls dressed as carrots were dancing at the bottom of the stage – it was brilliant and I love all that. Mind you, I should probably be getting some kind of cut from farmers, because I'm sure carrot sales must have gone up!'

Louis Tomlinson